To Da...d
that
Can
all the best Rachel

Copyright: Rachel Sambrooks 2017

Inside photography and pictures Rachel Sambrooks and Eve Hind
Cover photograph of Rachel Sambrooks by Joanna Steele.
Cover photography designed by Sameena Zehra.

LOTTERY FUNDED

Supported using public funding by

ARTS COUNCIL ENGLAND

Contents

Introduction

This book is a collection of poetry inspired by my maternal grandmother, some telling a story, some random responses, some snatches of memories.

My grandmother was born Edith Hind in 1911 but preferred to be called Eve, and signed her paintings as such. She wasn't a famous woman; she educated herself through books, gaining an interest in yoga, Zen and a love of cake. This collection is inspired by my memory of her life, but also is a personal perspective on the age old question 'where do we come from' and where are we going?

At Nan's funeral, the poem by Christina Rossetti quoted, "It is better to forget and smile than to remember and be sad."

I will remember and smile.

The show 'Stand By Your Nan' and this accompanying book has been supported using public funding by Arts Council England funding and is touring London community venues in 2017 with the producer Sameena Zehra.

Rachel Sambrooks

Clippy on the Buzzes

In the Birmingham accent, 'bus' sounds like 'buzz'.

Eve's ambition was to be a bus conductor or a 'clippy' on the buzz.

I want to be a clippy on the buzzes

That's the job for me

Nothing better than clipping the tickets

Checking them on and chucking the naughty boys off

Taking charge of the buzz. Going all over the shop, all over

Travelling about all day, with my clipping machine on my hip

Clip clip clip. Smiling at strangers that will soon be friends

Taking their coppers, as they ting to stop and I hang at the front

Chatting to Driver. We do have a laugh,

In my smart smart uniform all bristling and clean

I watch the clippy on the buzz as a passenger

He comes over, with his balanced ability

to navigate the aisles, like a panther or circus tightrope walker

He knows what to do, no messing about just

Clippity clip clip clip

I smile and thank him as he clips my ticket

He smells of old man and tobacco, and as he moves on, I think

That could be me. I could do that.

I could be a clippy on the buzz.

Hot Work

My grandmother worked in many jobs including a coat salesperson in John Lewis, but her trade was as a baker and chocolate cake decorator.

Hot work in the chocolate factory

Learning how to decorate

Tall icing bags, fingers grow strong and stubby

In the squeezing, twirling patterns over the tops

Of the Kunzle showboats, a cake chocolate

Sweetness licked onto fingers

Cake in her blood, in our blood

Fairy cakes always ready in a tub for sharing

Behind the scenes, the ends of tray bakes

Are rolled into chocolate pralines

A swirl of caramel, a hit of chocolate

How could anyone diet through that?

Mocking her gently for the attempt to diet at eighty-two

A slimline thin thin guru in a leotard

Grins out from the cover of a diet book

Splattered with cake mix

Rotund body doesn't fit the mould

And pages of writing down what you ate

Ends with daily treats

A tot of whisky, a small fairy cake

Not a beach body but

Warm, cosy hugging with softness

A cupcake body ready for sharing.

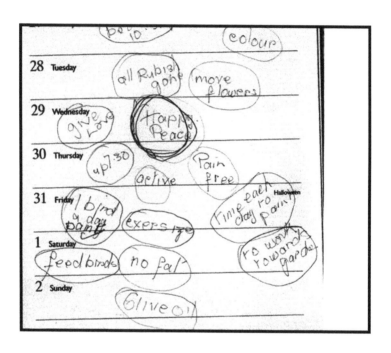

		colour
28 Tuesday	all Rubish gone	move flowers
29 Wednesday	give Love	Happy Peace
30 Thursday	up 7.30	Pain free
	active	
31 Friday	1 b/rd a day paint	exersize	Time each day to paint
1 Saturday			to work towards garden
	feed birds	no fat	
2 Sunday			
	Olive oil		

Halloween

7

Jade

Eve had a set of bookshelves she sat next to in the front room. On the top, she put green things she loved and called it her jade shelf.

The deep green ripples of a seabed reeds

The lucky talisman of healing

The aura of aurora borealis

A pint of green cabbage water

The gleam of Raphael

A lampshade from Homebase speaks of oriental mystery

Like a hand-painted parasol

And the small statue of an unknown man

Confucius, Nan, he's Confucius

Jade in the corner and the colour healing book

Colour of renewal, spring the best-loved season

New shoots, grass, green, rebirth.

Expeditions with Elsie

That summer, at the weekend, they took

The charabang coach trip on

Long treks over the Clent hills where later

Eve's ashes were scattered in bluebell woods

That summer

Their girls, all grandmothers now,

Blackberry picking and having fun

Taking a break at the pub, Eve and Elsie went inside

That summer

A row of girls under ten, now over 70,

Perched on the outside wall, drinking pop

Whilst Eve and Elsie drank in a midday pub crawl

That summer

Like free birds, summers of bread and wine

Sitting in bars you were banned from

Pub-crawling when you weren't allowed

That summer

Luckily the charabanc will take you home

Safe as you snooze through the booze.

Back-room Buddha

In the front room, the family came

On the face of it, she was ordinary

Taking egg and chips on a tray

In the back room, she painted

Eve signed at the bottom

Hidden under secrets, acrylics and oils

A circle of friends that no one knew

In the front room, her bookshelves

Filled with knowledge, a tot of coppers

Her jade statue of a man

Pointing to the moon

Pointing to the back room

In the back room, a view out onto garden

Lawned and veg grown, soil ground into fingers

Merged with cake mix and paint. Her hands speak volumes

Her hands that of a creator. Rooted.

Put your Leg in Bed

Put your leg in bed, she said, put your leg in bed

Top deck of the bus was scary; I'd never been on a bus to town

Only ever stayed downstairs near the door

But 'put your leg in bed' she said, put your leg in bed

I didn't know what she meant and frowned

She made a triangle with her arm at the elbow and

Gestured – put your arm in there, she said, put your leg in bed

So embarrassed (I was) but I did slip my arm through hers,

Worried that others would see and hear the accent

Though we all had it. Embarrassed at ancient phrasing

The 'any road up' and the 'nice bit of meat'

Put your leg in bed, she said, put your leg in bed

Got off at the Bullring market so she could buy her fish and veg

Hagglers shouting, a self-conscious attack on my nose by fish guts

Unlike the sea, more like scraping the bottom of an ice crate bin

Put your leg in bed, she said, put your leg in bed

No cars in a car park, no air-conditioned clean-lined

Supermarket and we walked around

Me, a child scared and out of place

Put your leg in bed, she said, put your leg in bed

Safe, arm in arm, I did.

Running for a Buzz

Can't miss the buzz but takes too long walking, yawning, stretch of pavement

Past the house where Olive lived, friend with the heat in her hands

And number 101 that held a young couple who argued in the street

And the community centre for street parties, Christmas dances, Jubilee

Her feet troubled the pavement, dashing faster

Skipping over dislodged paving stones and to the bottom,

Turning past the small run of small shops, but the buzz is already there

She'd never make it. Picked up her pace, running out of time, out of breath

Holding her hat on with one hand, in other the shopping trolley bag

Dragging behind her with bumps and bounces

Roadworks force a stench of hot tar filling her nostrils

She clenches them but carries on, the buzz her object of desire

Must catch it or wait for too long in the cold

Hitting bones through to the marrow, banging feet onto pavement

Eyes on and brain set in motion, ignored her feet

Tripped up, one betraying toe caught on

An upturned tectonic fault of paving sends her flying

Onto hot tar, searing into the skin of her chin

Sticking it together, making a scar that would forever be

In my mind a part of her face. Beautiful

In her mind, the scar of rash decisions

Of running when you shouldn't run, shouldn't climb shouldn't be.
Beautiful.

Transport

Where did the trams go? Trolley buses they were called

When Granddad had the panic attack

He held on to the rudder for dear life

Ting and *punch* went the ticket machine

Now I hear a beep as the card slips over yellow sun

A beep doubled up as a child takes their place on the platform

And the whizzing and the shuddering as the train pulls in

We live so close I can touch it

Race the train to catch it

Feet pound to beep in, jump on

Only a couple of minutes into the town

I can walk it but I don't

The trams came back to the town

And I dodged and weaved out the way, surprised

Like an ancient time traveller on an airport landing strip

And once upon a time, Nan rode in a motorbike side-car

Once upon a time, she swung round corners on the bus, hanging on for dear life

Once she walked to the shops, one foot in front of the other.

Back Then

Didn't have seat belts in the back

The teenagers crouched in the boot

Didn't have computer games or MP3

Music came on tape or vinyl or eight-track

Live meant you only heard it once

Diet pop with ice cubes and cheese and onion crisps

In the beer garden

Sat alone whilst the adults sat indoors and drank

Beer and wine. Feeling fine, they drove us home

The clink of the cubes against the side of the glass

The straw if you was lucky

And it would float and you wish it to stand up straight

Like in a milkshake

The tiny things tiny things

Like a ladybird on a fingernail

The adults missed it all

The ice cubes and the crisps

The straw floating in the glass

The swinging legs on the picnic bench in the beer garden

Strong grass takes a lot to pull

The bees. Far off. The fizz of the bubbles.

List Variations: Reasons to Diet

1. My mother said I was built like a battleship, with legs like tree trunks.
2. My grandmother was on the Rosemary Conley fat-free diet in her eighties, she bakes fat-free fairy cakes with added butter.
3. Always have a tray to carry food into your man.
4. Once I put my diary in the bin because my boyfriend read it. Perhaps this will go in the bin.
5. On holiday the calories don't count. This is also true of Christmas.
6. I always had seconds of Christmas dinner. Extra pigs in blankets. My mother smoked a cigarette in the kitchen whilst she cooked.

Variations i)

1. My mother tray bakes Rosemary Conley.
2. Once I put my mother in the bin. Maybe my boyfriends in the bin.
3. Always have a grandmother to carry food.
4. My fat-free diet at aged eight is on my tray.
5. The calories don't work, they just make it worse.
6. Once I put my pigs in blankets on the cigarettes whilst I cooked my boyfriend.
7. My diet has a cigarette.

Variations ii)

1. My mother said battleships built with the tree trunks never float the boat of a boyfriend.
2. Always have a tray to hand in case you have to batter your mother.
3. Men like trays.
4. You better learn to do housework or find a man that likes housework. Good luck with that.
5. Once I put my tray in the bin.
6. Cigarette whilst cooking counts as a meal. Carry the cigarette on a tray to your man.
7. Egg and chips do not count as one of your five a day.

When I am an Old Lady

When I am an old lady

I won't wear purple, I'll wear a bikini

The costume not the atoll

Though I shall be the size of a small island

When I am an old lady

I will eat cake until I am the size of a house

Fill the interior of a three-bed semi

And it takes two helicopters to airlift me to my funeral

When I am an old lady

I will blow raspberries

And pull faces at the other old ladies

Who are outfoxed as they try to grimace

But are too botoxed

When I am an old lady

I will have to sport a name badge of the sort

That says 'Don't call me Nan'

But if my kids' kids, can call me 'Gran Master Flash'

Hashtag you old toad

As I greet them in my bikini

Drinking Martini by the truckload.

In Shed World

In the man cave
Is a Portakabin of testosterone
Glorious mdf bar
Chemical toilet
Cinema

In the woman shed
Is a mannequin wearing a flowery tabard
No chair, staring straight ahead
Doing the ironing
Bored

No one told Virginia Woolf
Her kitchen staff wanted rooms of their own
With doors that shut
And the mannequin wants
A writer's hut.

Harpy

In the gilded cage, it screeched again
He wondered when his budgie had grown so big

Feathers pressed against the bars, flicking out from the gaps
Quill falling to the floor

Anvil beak scrapes against metal
Tarnished and burnished, flaking off fake gold coating

Kept growing each day, choking against the tightening bars
Creaking stainless steel pressing against harpy's feathered wing bone

No space left, eating scraps fed from cold cold room
Thrown from afar

The walls bulged outwards
The cage burst slowly
The cage burst

And whilst the Harpy saw escape, it didn't move
Still thought itself pretty polly, still waiting for the gaze

Cawing for crumbs, cage in tatters at its feet
But Harpy was harpy and he didn't look anymore.

Eternal Present Moment

Educating adults in the flow of love and light with books, and art and dance, the opera is local, the concerts free, the library open, and my Eve Hind starts painting at fifty-five.

Art is life and life is art and paint is paper and art is paint and paint is colour and colour is healing and healing is wholeness and the wholeness is all and all is art and art is life

The phoenix rises whilst hollow men drew lines in the sand

She paints flowers and people, dark circles for nostrils off kilter, paths through the forest, petals on the flowers, the garden, a landscape, a still life more and more until the caked on paint layers thick in the upstairs room, walls coated with furniture, no space left now and everyone gone, she moves down to the back room, where once she spoke to the dead and now alive, she thrives in eternal present moment.

She struggles and flows, she strokes the canvas abstract, flowing moments of emotion until the paintings become unfinished and the hand

And the hand

can't pick up the brush for long.

> She paints a self portrait. There she is as the
> enlightened one, as her own Buddha, in her

eternal present moment.

Like the paint on her hands, like the apron flour dusted, like the sticky flour hands, like the wonders of the larder, like gorillas in the mist, like the tree trunks rotting, like the wind speed dropping.

Conversation

Do you remember the little dog? No.
The little dog I had, it sat on my shelf in a basket and you
Asked me what it was made from
It was seal skin, so old it was back when they made things

From skin
Sat in a basket
A one-eyed tiny little Pomeranian
A basket with red felt

Bald where you'd petted it, rubbed its head, pretended it was
real
Well loved
The seal fur rubbed away, loved so much its fur turned to shiny
leather
And when you were older because you asked I told you
It's made from seal skin, baby seal

You asked me for the dog and you lost it
You don't remember where you put it

Jumping up and down for coins to pay for the ice cream van
Always wanting for something

Do you remember the little dog? Where's he gone now?
Which charity shop, which junk shop, which skip did he go to?

Eve – the First and Last

Eve like the first women, changed from Edith
Like that you were mercurial and flexible
Adventurous with the times
Now no water allowed, nil by mouth
On the hospital bedside table, tall

A pot of Vaseline, greasy, peeling label
Decades old like
The marmite, the cake tins, the eggs
I dabbed it onto tissue and her rough lost lips

Through tiny cracked mouth
Thank you, she said
Another dab of Vaseline and that was done
Thank you, she said
Bless you

I don't know if anyone else gave her Vaseline after that
The only gift I could give her was dotted onto rough skin
Bless you, she said, her last words to me
Bless you and thank you.

Better You Should Forget and Smile

I am sad at her passing.
My mother tells the minister to 'have a word' with me
As I am likely to show emotion

Oh no, don't do that, never show it, don't be a fuss
In a room of elderly ladies who will all go soon
We need to be happy and believe she's with Jesus now
We can't miss an old lady
We can't see them as meaningful
Just let the light fade out and be blessed
She was old and had a 'good innings'
Even though she never played cricket
Old means she was lucky
Didn't die in war or famine or childbirth
She survived a century
And for that you must be glad, and quip about
Her length of life

But don't you see, a life can be missed even if it is long
Because in the present moment, she is gone.

Gifts

Olive had the heat in her hands
Gifts we kept back from sharing
Secret coven of white witches
Don't tell in case you are shown up
Beaten out of you
Locked up in the sanatorium
Don't tell about the ghosts
Don't tell
Automatic writing
Painting
The Golden One visiting.
Pass it on, whisper, pass it on

By Heart

I memorised your face, all wrinkles all lines but they faded

Like the sound of your voice

You left tapes but on them are lectures by others you listened to

Not your voice

The only sound of you is footsteps in the background

As you changed the tapes as you walked across the room

To turn it over in the ways we did way back then

The sound of slow sure steps, across the room

I know it was the back room and you were sat in your armchair

Next to the glass cabinet of ornaments

We weren't allowed to touch, glasses and plates

Never use the nice stuff. Just for show, and behind you

Was the window to the garden that you tended

All weathers until nearly a century old

And I can see you listening to the tape and realising one side had reached the end

You stood and walked over to the recorder

Saying nothing, you turned it over and clicked record again

I hear the voice of the lecturer but all I have of you

Is footsteps

Why didn't you just say hello?

Did you not know one day I would be desperate to hear it again

4700 – the number of your phone, you said that when you picked it up

4700 – I hear them again in my head I remember

But still what I wouldn't give for you to have recorded yourself

Reciting poetry or saying hello, one more time

But you stayed quiet not feeling important enough or public enough to record it

And all I have is footsteps and a memory of a number off by heart.

Thank you to my Nan, my family and to all those who have shared their grandmother stories as part of this journey.

Eve, with her daughter and great grand-daughter. 2001.

Lightning Source UK Ltd.
Milton Keynes UK
UKHW011835140919
349778UK00001B/27/P